F L Y W A T E R

F L Y W A T E R

GRANT McCLINTOCK AND MIKE CROCKETT

LYONS & BURFORD, NEW YORK

LYONS & BURFORD, 31 WEST 21ST STREET, NEW YORK CITY, NY 10010

LIBRARY OF CONGRESS CATALOGING-IN-PUBLICATION DATA
MCCLINTOCK, GRANT.
FLYWATER / GRANT MCCLINTOCK AND MIKE CROCKETT.
ISBN 1-55821-339-2
1. FLY FISHING — PICTORIAL WORKS. 2. FLY FISHING — WEST (U.S.)
— PICTORIAL WORKS. 3. FLY FISHING — BRITISH COLUMBIA — PICTORIAL WORKS.
I. CROCKETT, MIKE. II. TITLE.
SH456.M35   1994
799. 1'755—DC20   94-25931 CIP

PREVIOUS PAGE: THE NATURE CONSERVANCY STRETCH OF SILVER CREEK IS SUCH
AN ELOQUENT EXPRESSION OF FLYWATER THAT ALL OTHER FORMS OF FISHING ARE
NOT ONLY INADVISABLE BUT ALSO ILLEGAL.

DESIGNED BY CAROL HARALSON

PRINTED IN ITALY

FLYWATER IS THE PLAYING FIELD OF THE FLY

FISHERMAN — THAT WATER WHICH CAN BE

SUCCESSFULLY AND ENJOYABLY FISHED WITH A

FLY ROD. AND ALTHOUGH FLY FISHERMEN CAST

OVER THE MOST IMPROBABLE SORTS OF WATER,

TRUE FLYWATER IS BUT A SMALL FRACTION OF

THE WHOLE — A RESTRICTION WHICH FLY

FISHERMEN NOT ONLY ACCEPT BUT ACTUALLY

EMBRACE AS A DEFINING ELEMENT OF THE SPORT.

CONTENTS

FISHHEAD

MIKE CROCKETT

Eight years ago, I had never been fly fishing in my life—a life, incidentally, which at that point was going extremely well: business was thriving, I had a beautiful wife, two great kids and another on the way, a vacation house in the mountains, wonderful friends, just about everything I had ever wanted and more than I expected. I spent very little time worrying about all the ways such a life might go bad. And then, in the same week my daughter Julia was born, I received a devastating medical diagnosis. Those lumps I had noticed were not caused by some infection but were an incurable form of lymphoma. I remember first trying to avoid, but then finally asking, the usual question—"How long do I have, Doctor?"

As anyone who has experienced this horror can testify, the medical profession answers this question with a bias not toward hope, but rather against creating unreasonable expectations. At some point after treatment had begun, the traditional euphemism was offered—it would be wise to get my affairs in order.

After the initial shock wave passed, I realized that I had actually received some rather unsurprising news: I was going to die sometime. That it seemed likely to be sooner rather than later merely intensified my focus on the implication: I didn't have time to waste. In a process that would benefit even the perfectly healthy, I began taking inventory and realized I was involved in a lot of activity I didn't really enjoy. Guided by a will I hadn't experienced before, I came to a decision. Although it was clearly not possible to be always happy, it should be possible to be content with one's choices of activities. I started to uncover aspects of my life that had nothing to do with present fulfillment, but were simply stubborn holdovers from an earlier time, activities which I had wandered through in an unengaged daze. This approach now seemed suddenly absurd. Becoming a fly fisherman was not the most profound change growing from these revelations, but it made a lot more sense to me than, say, my golf game, which I discarded when I realized that fly fishing brought pleasure and contentment on every outing.

Like many recent arrivals to the fly fishing craze, I had a boyhood exposure to a more primitive form of fishing. For a couple of glorious summers, many an afternoon was spent with my little brother Jim on Aunt Maud's farm ponds in pursuit of the bass, bluegills, catfish, tadpoles and crayfish that populated the place. We generally warmed up on the small pond by landing a few crawdads with a string and pieces of raw bacon. The equipment for the real fishing was a cane pole with a red and white bobber. The bait was the earthworm freshly dug from the back yard before the hike to Aunt Maud's. We would watch the bobbers with one eye and the water moccasins slithering around the pond with the other eye. Jim and I had our fishing success—even today I can remember the feeling of slipping into sleep with images of the red and white float being pulled under by some fish of unknowable proportions. This pleasant sleep was only occasionally disturbed by dreams of water moccasin attacks.

After those early angling experiences, there followed a thirty-year period (which seems shockingly brief in retrospect) during which most decisions, whether trivial or momentous, seemed to be dictated, however indirectly, by considerations of sex and romance. Somehow fishing never came into play in this formula. Then, too, there was the inertia one begins to experience at a certain age: too old for new tricks, content with the mediocre skills attained in other recreational pursuits, disinclined toward further embarrassment as a rookie. These kinds of concerns were, for me, rendered inconsequential by the aforementioned visits to the doctor's office, and I began to see the opportunity to try something new as the essence of living.

During a trip to Colorado a few months after the cancer diagnosis, I prevailed upon a friend to introduce me to fly fishing on the San Miguel River. It would be hard to imagine a more beautiful place for an escape or a healing experience than this small freestone river flowing through red sandstone canyon walls and mixed forests of blue spruce, cottonwood, and alders. In its upper stretches, the San Miguel is a brook trout fishery, and after a couple of frustrating days, I could handle the equipment well enough to engage a few of these beautiful and high-spirited fish. I was still a tragically inadequate technician, but I was escaping gravity by riding a steep learning curve, well on my way to becoming a fully-addicted fishhead.

In those days of an uncertain and worrisome future, I gradually became aware of a very interesting phenomenon—virtually every minute on the stream was spent in relaxed contentment. Fishing— fly fishing— was the only enterprise I was involved in that transported me away from the considerable anxieties I felt about the difficulties that were lurking. Occasionally, it even served as an effective relief for physical pain or nausea. In time, I began to see fishing as a form of therapy. I didn't think about it much then, but I have come to understand that the therapeutic value came from the concentration required to fish properly, especially with a dry fly, and from the magnificent environment where the fishing takes place. The constant challenge of the next pool, a different fly, a better cast, and the sensory load of visual beauty and cool flowing water leave no place for extraneous thoughts. The activity of rigging up, wading,

casting, watching the line unfold and following the float of the fly—it all flows together to become a kind of meditation, a spiritual recreation. So, that first summer, when I began to see fly fishing as good tasting medicine, I always had a serviceable excuse to head for the river, and I took advantage of it.

Today, eight years after first picking up a fly rod, I have passed two death sentence dates given by the doctors who didn't want to create false hopes, although the path was not one of steady improvement. Half a dozen courses of chemotherapy and several surgeries and hospitalizations failed to arrest the disease; I was pronounced "drug resistant." Finally, I travelled to Stanford University Medical Center for an experimental treatment with monoclonal antibodies that had been developed specifically for me over the preceding three years. There were no guarantees, but the treatment had some promise, and I was optimistic it would be my salvation. The treatment would take almost two months, so my wife Andy and I moved into an apartment near the hospital. After some initial tests we received a report for which we were unprepared: for only the second time in over fifty such individual trials, the antibody no longer reacted with my cells, and there was no reason to pursue the treatment. Although there were some other rather esoteric experimental treatments available, my best hope was gone.

We decided to make the best of things, and spend the rest of the summer in Colorado. Among other things, we could do some trout fishing—a lot of trout fishing—in the San Miguel River. I knew from my few previous days of fishing that the river would provide a much needed escape from reality.

Two months later, when we returned to Oklahoma, I saw my doctor again. I knew before the exam that I was much better. I knew already that three years of steady decline had been reversed. He couldn't offer any medical explanation for this unusual remission, but he did suggest that I should keep doing whatever it was I had been doing that summer. And, of course, I have. I've had no medical treatment or symptoms since.

I don't mean to suggest that fly fishing can cure cancer. When conventional medicine failed me, I tried every alternative approach that came to my attention. It is possible that any or even all of them made some contribution; it is significant to me that many of the non-traditional therapeutic techniques as I understood them sought to produce in the patient the same state of mind that came so effortlessly for me in the trout stream. I can say this: fly fishing, more than any other activity, frees my mind and nourishes my soul. And I do know that time spent on the river has often provided a profound sense of well-being—that feeling of being rooted in the present without needs or worries beyond the moment. Whether there is any connection between my time as a fisherman and my current state of good health is neither knowable nor ultimately important—the rewards that come to the fly fisherman are evident and sufficient. But I will always believe that fly fishing has affected my life in a very positive way, and that I carry with me much that I have learned and felt astream. There is an old saying that one can never enter the same river twice. The river is always new; the man is forever changed.

Two summers ago, Andy and I were visiting our friends Grant and Paula McClintock in Ketchum, Idaho. After a fine day of fishing on the Big Wood River and a pleasant cocktail hour, we somehow began discussing the project which became this book. The next morning, unlike so many such discussions, it still seemed like a good idea. Later, we enlisted Jack Hemingway—a devoted and skilled outdoorsman with a long and rich experience in fly fishing (and with the stamina of a man half his age). What followed was a memorable year of fishing that can best be portrayed by the photographs in this book. It may not be possible for Grant's images of western flywater and fly fishing to provide as much enjoyment as we experienced in a series of superb fishing trips, but we hope they will help the fisherman through the long winter and give the non-fisherman a better understanding of why some of us are obsessed to the point we freely answer to the name "fishhead."

TELLURIDE, COLORADO
SPRING 1994

A FISHERMAN'S LIFE

JACK HEMINGWAY

I have always found it impossible to write about the things I love to do in a place where they can easily be done. The passion inherent in the pursuit of these activities seems to preclude any need to write about them. This is certainly true of fly fishing. In the places where I live, for the most part the fishing is nearby. That is why I live there. In these places I must write about fishing in the off season when the pull of several waters can no longer tempt me.

At this moment, at an artist's tilted work desk in a rented house in San Miguel de Allende, thoughts of fishing come easily, unemcumbered by the possibility of leaving the work for moments astream. From here I will try to impart to you what fly fishing has meant to me. The opportunity to do this I owe to two fine friends, Mike Crockett and Grant McClintock, whose project this book truly is. For all three of us, the making of this book has been a true labor of love. It is intended to give pleasure to the eye and to the mind and, we hope, to the heart as well.

The lifetime of a fly fisher, like all serious interests, has its spring, its summer and autumn, and, eventually, its ending in winter. I will attempt to give you a summary of the seasons of my own fishing life with the hope that some might benefit from my experiences and avoid repeating my errors.

The spring of my fishing life began in the West, at the L-Bar-T dude ranch in the valley of the Clark's Fork of the Yellowstone. My father had the wisdom to let me build up a desire to fish on my own without pushing me in any way and for the greater part of that summer of my sixth year, I simply watched him. Then finally I was permitted to try for myself with some of his old backup equipment. A pond with some lovely little eastern brook trout and a back eddy of the Clark's Fork near the cabin became my haunts for the last few weeks of our stay. Though I used a fly rod and line, I threaded morning-caught grasshoppers on old worn-out wet flies my father had discarded. I learned that the back eddy would sink the baited fly if I let it float naturally around until the vortex pulled it down. This was almost invariably followed by a hesitation of the line movement and an overstrong strike on my part, sending a small golden-hued cutthroat trout over my head to land behind me. There I would pounce on it and put it in one of the Hardy Brothers woven grass bags that my father used for creels in those days. On the other hand, the pond proved frustrating, but those beautiful brookies with their white-edged pectorals remain a vision to be remembered in my winter dreams. In those first few years of fishing at the ranch my objective was to catch lots of trout. Whatever fish Papa didn't want for breakfast were welcomed at the kitchen of the L-Bar-T.

The second of these early seasons witnessed my conversion from grasshoppers to wet flies, the method employed by my father. It was his basic wet fly technique, casting down and across with silk lines and tapered gut leaders nine feet long with two or more flies premounted on droppers in addition to the tippet fly. It served me well, and I was soon catching more and slightly larger fish than I had with the hoppers. I had also become more mobile, riding my horse further and further afield to explore and fish lakes, ponds, and streams throughout the area.

The gift of a book from my stepfather set the stage for further development. The book was *Trout* by Ray Bergman. I still recommend it to friends. It completely captured my imagination and, besides opening the doors to vast new spheres of places to fish and techniques to master, it stimulated a voracious hunger in me to read all the fly-fishing literature I could lay my hands on. Little did I realize what a pleasant and rewarding enterprise this would become. First the American authors and then the British fed those ever-present winter dreams.

This springtime of my fishing life continued into my late teens and being sent to prep school back East in the Hudson Highlands did not interfere with my progress. I began to develop a certain skill in upstream low-water worming in the little brooks that ran through the Black Rock Forest. Indeed, it was there that I discovered the possibilities of upstream nymphing (without the travesty of an indicator) in the few stretches of those tiny streams adequate to the purpose. Numbers of fish caught continued to have some importance, but my father's early admonition never to waste any fish or game established my limits. The concept of catch and release had not been disseminated beyond Michigan, where a few fishermen experimented with the Hazzard plan first instituted by Trout Unlimited, and the Paradise in Belfort, Pennsylvania. I had not yet heard of this idea and was much too busy learning and honing my skills to worry about anything more than finding new fishing grounds holding more and bigger fish.

Yellowstone National Park and the area around it became my new nirvana. When I was sixteen, my mother and stepfather, Paul Mowrer, gave me a used Pontiac which I was allowed to drive from Chicago to join them at the Crossed Sabers dude ranch west of Cody, Wyoming. Having the car enabled me to broaden my horizons well beyond the nearby waters of the Shoshone River and its tributaries. A friendly fly fisherman also vacationing at the Crossed Sabers helped me along by giving me some bi-

visible dry flies and a few pointers on line handling during the drift and retrieve. He was just one of many helpful fisherman I have met over the years. He encouraged me to try the dries on the big water of the main Shoshone, and there I had my first few successes.

But the clincher came when I drove into the park and had my first session of dry fly fishing on the Madison. The stretch I chose has seldom produced well for me since, but that day it was to provide a magic moment. I chose fast water, with which I was familiar from the freestone Shoshone but here it had a dark bottom lent by the volcanic rocks and, of course, verdant weed beds wherever the current slackened along the sides of the run. I had read George LaBranche's *The Dry Fly and Fast Water* and, following the author's dictates, began to fish the current methodically, false casting between drifts. In the shallow water at the head of the run my fly disappeared in the swirl created by what seemed to me to be the biggest trout I had ever seen. My reaction was slow because of my surprise, and consequently I did not strike too fast and the fish was on. He turned out to be no bigger that the cutthroat my mother, Paul, and I had caught on wet flies along the shores of Yellowstone Lake and on the upper Yellowstone River above the Lake. But what a difference in strength and excitement. It was my first brown trout over fourteen inches and, though he was an ugly hook-jawed male, he looked beautiful to me—all eighteen inches of him, his spots Ming red in the afternoon sun.

Another angler who helped me develop my skills was Leander McCormick, author of *Fishing Around the World*. He spent part of an afternoon helping me with my casting and taught me something which was to prove invaluable over the years—steeple casting, in which the back cast is thrown as close as possible to straight up before the forward stroke. Practicing this helps anyone to keep a high back cast, the hallmark of all good casters.

The dry fly became an obsession after that first brown on the Madison, and I think that I had caught the big fish bug as well. I suppose that I had begun to enter the summer of my fly fisher's life.

The following year saw my introduction to Silver Creek in Idaho. My father's accounts of Silver Creek in his letters to me at school were up to the mark. It truly did resemble the English chalk stream I had dreamed about while reading and rereading Halford's *Dry Fly Fishing*. The problem was that my skills were not up to the difficulty it presented. My first try was with a young guide, Clayton Stuart, who years later became mayor of Sun Valley. Stu was one of a fine crew of local fly fishermen recruited by head guide Taylor Williams. The guides knew the locale well but were limited by what we would now view as inadequate tackle and limited knowledge of aquatic entomology. Quite frankly, this was true of most trout fishermen of that time, and although he did all he could, Stu could not create a situation which would assure my success on Silver Creek—especially as I was determined to fish only dry fly. He recommended three patterns to me on that occasion: Woodruff (insect green wool body, grizzly hackle tip tail, brown hackle tied full and grizzly hackle-tip spent wings on #12 or #14 hook), the then-ubiquitous ginger quill on the same size hooks, and the Renegade (a possibility which I rejected out of hand—probably a mistake, as it does a fair job of imitating an egg-laying caddis).

I remember on that first foray creeping up to a point just below a *U* bend where an old fencepost in the middle of the stream had gathered weeds that hung below it in the current. There were multiple rises both above and below the post, and Stu assured me that some of those rises were three- to five-pound rainbows. Try as I would, I could not fool those fish. The flies I was using certainly didn't look much like what was floating down the stream, although the ginger quill wasn't that far off the mark except for being much too big. Apparently there were times when those flies produced but not then and not for me.

I still see Stu now and again, and he is kind enough to recall that, despite my lack of success, he had felt I was an accomplished caster. Looking back on those days, I see some positive aspects about the tackle limitations. For one, the necessity of false casting to dry the fly, if done properly and well out of the fish's sight periphery, rested the fish to some extent. The need to keep the gut leader properly dampened and to stop fishing altogether for periods of ten minutes to half an hour to wipe off, sun dry and regrease the fine silk lines gave the angler a chance to sit and observe what was happening in and on the water and to appreciate the magical natural world around him. The finest leaders available then were 4x gut and were not as strong as the 8x used now. One needed to make a

much better presentation to avoid drag, and to handle any hooked fish exceedingly carefully. Needless to say, very few large fish were landed, especially in weed-infested streams such as Silver Creek. When they were landed, luck was required combined with a level of skill seldom achieved by our modern-day anglers.

Those last couple of years before World War II were accented for me by numerous wonderful new fly fishing experiences. A six-week idyll in Yellowstone country with several of my prep school classmates is described in some detail in my *Misadventures of a Fly Fisherman*. Many pointers we followed came from a fabulous little book we bought in a West Yellowstone tackle shop, *Waters of Yellowstone* by Howard Back. It has since been replaced by a more up-to-date version by Charles Brooks, with photos by my friend Dan Callaghan. We all grew in sophistication. We had brought along fly tying equipment as well as a supply of eastern dry fly patterns from Darbees in Livingston Manor, New York, purchased with our allowances. Paul Stroud, a well-known fly tyer in Arlington Heights, Illinois, had helped me learn new tying skills and prior to our departure gave me a supply of the then-new leader material, nylon. Paul had dyed it brown with silver nitrate, and it suited the Yellowstone streams perfectly. It was much stronger than gut, although somewhat unreliable and prone to surprise breaks when cold, nicked, or badly knotted. (I remember a particularly frustrating day at the Widow's Preserve, hooking enormous brook trout and being broken time after time even with our damsel flies tied onto the butt of the leader.)

Later that summer on a weekend away from my temporary job at Hines lumber mill in central Oregon, I had my first experience with summer steelhead on the North Umpqua. I had learned about this river by devouring the chapter devoted to it in Ray Bergman's book. I was able to raise a fish to the fly, but it was almost immediately broken off. One of my companions had his prized Granger Aristocrat fly rod confiscated by a state trooper who found he was fishing without a license. The river captured our imaginations for its beauty, its power, and the magnificent fish we knew it harbored.

The war years following that last war-free summer for young Americans supplied occasional moments for fly fishing. Much to the amusement of my military fellows, once I had become an officer I took advantage of my new privileges by taking basic fly tackle with me wherever I went—including occupied France, where I was sent on a parachute mission. There I had several opportunities to ply my craft, one of them hair-raising. A German patrol came by while I was fishing!

The immediate post-war years saw a return to the West. On the campus of the University of Montana my continuing education included fly fishing between classes. I learned about positive drag with dry flies— that is, specially designed dry flies cast cross-current and allowed to swim around below while dragging along the surface leaving a small wake. This technique was used locally with hard-bodied horsehair imitations of giant stoneflies during the famous salmon fly hatch. Later it proved effective with smaller damsel fly patterns on Silver Creek and in Germany while fishing for grayling and brown trout on the Eder River and the lower Ammer in Bavaria. My return to the Army and Europe followed several years of tying flies for a living in San Francisco. I also worked for a fishing line company, first in its home office in Rhode Island and then at sportsmen's shows doing demonstration casting. Later I travelled the West Coast selling the dubious virtues of the new over-the-rod spinning reel— the cause of the great fishing revolution of the twentieth century.

Had it not been for the advent of the fixed spool (spinning) reel in the United States after World War II, it is quite possible that sport fishing, and trout fishing in particular, would never have experienced the explosion of interest and participation it has enjoyed. Spinning tackle made instant experts of everyone in the country who had been previously unable to cast a bait-casting reel without backlash or a fly rod without catching bushes and trees. Spinning made casting easy and, I must admit, I was induced to give it a try. It was great fun to cast light-weight lures tremendous distances—to reach fish previously out of reach. In much the same way, many of today's fly anglers have been seduced by the relative ease with which extraordinary success can be achieved with deep drifted wet flies and nymphs beneath an indicator. Guides have promoted this method as the easiest path to success for their customers. I am biased, of course, but I consider the technique, like spinning, a method for fish hogs. Its main attraction is easy success at the expense of the fishery and of other anglers. The idea of sport in fly fishing has been strained by the enormous improvements in quality of tackle. Methods which circumvent the ideals of sport and its inherent difficulties defeat all that is best about the sport. When I later realized the damage spinning was doing to our great fisheries all over the country, I rued the day I had decided to participate in its introduction. Fortunately, many others felt as I did, and two groups formed to protect and enhance our cold water fisheries. Trout Unlimited, which had existed for some time, became national in scope and aimed its efforts at saving the resources themselves. The newcomer, the Federation of Fly Fishermen, worked to convert the heathens to fly fishing.

These important activities were developing during the early 60s, at about the same time I first met a man who was to become my closest and best fishing companion. Dan Callaghan, then a recently married young attorney with the same sort of fiendish devotion to steelhead fly fishing that I was developing, became my companion on innumerable fishing expeditions all over the country and overseas as well. His photographic skills and organizational ability were vital in the formation of one of the strongest member clubs of the Federation of Fly Fishermen, the North Umpqua Steamboaters. My fishing in the early 1960s was limited to vacations and extended weekends due to family and business responsibilities. I have to admit that my failure to be a world beater in business was due in no small part to the fact that the world of fly fishing was infinitely more important to me than mundane matters of economic survival.

After my return to the Army and my tour in Europe I left active duty and settled my family in Portland, Oregon, close to the scene of my first successes with steelhead fishing, the Kalama River in southwest Washington. Many other fine steelhead rivers were nearby as well. Merrill Lynch sent me to New York for training that was followed by an assignment in Havana. But a bad case of hepatitis and the arrival of Fidel Castro in Havana led to my transfer to San Francisco—within weekend reach of good fishing and close to reasonable winter steelhead fishing, including the North Umpqua.

The balance of the summer of my fishing life started with a permanent move to Idaho and the Big Wood River valley. I built a home along the river, five miles out of town, being careful to keep it well away from the flood plain. The next years were spent learning all that I could about two rivers, the Big and Little Wood. Of course this was interspersed with annual expeditions to the Yellowstone area with Dan Callaghan. I had finally learned to practice what I already knew to be the proper course of action. An hour spent sitting unobtrusively below what appeared to be a feeding flat beside a fallen tree in the Firehole River lead to a fantastically successful session with big rainbows and browns on emerging caddis. The lesson was that an approach during a feeding spree can easily put fish down, but careful fishing, once the frenzy has started, is unlikely to do so. I was still learning.

Selective Trout was published by Swisher and Richards in 1971 and it became a significant factor in awakening new interest in fly fishing. It was the first popularly presented work on trout stream insects and how best to emulate them with flies since Ernie Schwiebert's *Matching the Hatch,* which had come out too early to gain so wide an audience. Dan and I were privy to Swisher and Richards's explorations and also to work being done in Montana by fish biologist Dick Vincent. His work finally gave scientific credence to what serious trout fishermen already knew instinctively—that wild trout were superior to hatchery-reared trout in their ability to survive in the wild, with the glaring exception that, because of their territoriality, the larger mature fish had difficulty surviving the pervasive schooling tactics of hatchery trout dumped into their environment. Dan and I, along with another pal, Frank Moore, were appointed to our respective state fish and game commissions. There we were able to influence the gradual institution of wild fish programs in those areas where they were appropriate—permitting the hatcheries to concentrate their efforts on supplying urban fishing areas, reservoirs, and the growing anadromous fish programs.

My true maturity as a fly fisherman was, I feel, achieved by time spent in the desert on the Little Wood. It was one of the first streams in our part of the state to receive fry plants of brown trout, and I was like a mother hen keeping track of their development. I had my first eighteen-incher and my first twenty-four-incher mounted, but after that I stopped any killing, though several trophies of thirty inches fell to my hoppers over

the years. Unfortunately, despite a three-mile-long, fly-only catch-and-release area, the quality of trophy fishing has not held up, due to heavy bait fishing throughout the drainage. Nevertheless, there is a self-sustaining population of both wild browns and rainbows. And the possibility of a whopper still exists for the careful, thoughtful, skill-honed fly fisherman. Spending time on the stream, not just fishing but sitting and observing, can bring immense rewards in an appreciation of all the factors which play a role in a stream's ecology. The seemingly barren lava badlands along the Little Wood reveal an ecology teeming with wildlife. To see it, all that is required is time, quiet, and being always non-threatening.

Expeditions in the autumn of my fishing life have ranged farther afield, to the area around Lewiston, Idaho, to fish the great steelhead tributaries of the Snake River where it leaves the state and wends through the eastern Washington desert to the great Columbia. There we also hunted chukar and hungarian partridge. British Columbia drew us for the same reasons with ruffed grouse replacing partridge but giant steelhead still the main objective. Over the years we had come to use floating lines for these noble fish most of the time and, more and more frequently, dry flies fished with the skating technique I had first learned when a student in Montana. Our hooking success was enhanced by a few tricks, such as a loop between the reel and rod hand to help give sufficient slack on a tight line for the fly to be sucked into the fish's jaw. There is always something new to learn.

An improvement in my finances enabled me to devote some serious efforts in the pursuit of Atlantic salmon. Steelhead skills proved to be quite adequate, but salmon fishing developed some new techniques which proved valuable in their turn for steelheading. Most steelheaders scoff at the long two-handed fly rods used by many European salmon fishermen. These steelheaders are missing the point. Once the two-handed casting is mastered, it is infinitely less tiring over a long day's fishing, covers much more water efficiently, can be used where there is no room for a back cast and, importantly, causes no loss in the enjoyment of the fight.

Now seventy and in the mid-autumn of my fishing life, though I still look forward to great new experiences, I have a tendency to look back as well. I realize what enormous changes I have seen and, to a considerable extent, have participated in.

I can only hope that those who read this book and enjoy the beauty of its photographs will in turn take their place among those who truly love and support the sport of fly fishing. Despite its sometimes paralyzing excitement, fly fishing remains essentially a contemplative pastime without the taint of competitiveness we tend to bring to so many activities. I hope this book helps illuminate some of the qualities of this extraordinary pursuit.

SAN MIGUEL DE ALLENDE, MEXICO

SPRING 1994

F L Y W A T E R

Gallatin River

TO BE SUDDENLY CONNECTED THROUGH A RAINBOW ARC OF ROD AND RUN OF LINE TO SOMETHING AS PURELY WILD AS GOD'S OWN TROUT PRODUCES ASTONISHMENT AT THE CELLULAR LEVEL AND, AT LEAST FOR A MOMENT, BLURS THE BORDER BETWEEN MAN AND NATURE. IT IS A BOND WHICH RENEWS ITSELF TIME AFTER TIME AND IS THE ADDICTIVE ESSENCE OF THE SPORT.

Grayling Creek, Montana

St. Joe River, Idaho

THE TYING OF KNOTS MAY NOT BE FLY FISHING'S MOST COMPELLING ACTIVITY, BUT IF THE CAST IS THE HEART OF THE SPORT, THE KNOT IS SOMETHING LIKE THE PANCREAS — NOT TOO ROMANTIC BUT TRY TO DO WITHOUT ONE.

KNOTS, LIKE SO MANY THINGS, COME IN TWO SORTS — USEFUL AND WORTHLESS. USEFUL KNOTS ARE INTENDED, AND WHEN PROPERLY TIED BY THE FISHERMAN, HOLD HIS WORLD TOGETHER. WORTHLESS KNOTS ARE TIED BY THE WINDS, GENERAL INCOMPETENCE, AND BAD LUCK. THESE CAUSE STRESSED LINES TO BREAK AND FISHING TO CEASE. GOOD KNOTS GO BY NAMES SUCH AS BLOOD, TURLE, CLINCH. AMONG EVIL INTRUDERS ONE MIGHT ENCOUNTER ARE WIND, BIRD'S NEST, GRANNY.

DEALING EFFECTIVELY WITH THE UNINTENDED KNOT REQUIRES THE APPLICATION OF BUT THREE RULES:

1. NEVER TRY TO CAST YOUR WAY OUT OF A KNOT PROBLEM.
2. WHEN UNDOING UNWANTED KNOTS, EXPAND ANY LOOP YOU ENCOUNTER.
3. OFTEN IT'S WISE TO CUT AND START OVER.

AN IMPORTANT AUXILIARY RULE: EVEN THE MOST HAM-HANDED, BOOZE-ADDLED FISHING GUIDE IS POSSESSED OF A MYSTERIOUS ABILITY (FAR BEYOND YOUR OWN) TO DEAL WITH OBNOXIOUS KNOTS.

Wind knot, The Madison

Fish signs

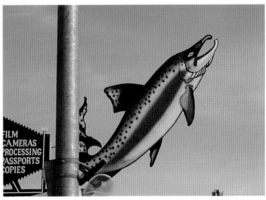

Emerson wrote, "I think no virtue goes with size." Emerson must not have done much fishing. If not virtuous, size is certainly satisfying, while an extreme lack of size is, well . . . amusing.

Frank Smethurst, Fishhead

Asking a fly fisherman how he got started in the sport usually elicits a fairly predictable story about a creek here or a pond there, about a Grandpa mentor or a country uncle. But every now and then one hears a tale with a difference.

Frank Smethurst grew up in Georgia, and his family had a swimming pool which was allowed to go natural during the winter, forming lots of algae. Frank thought this looked like a good fishing hole in which to try out his first fly rod. He hand stocked it with half a dozen bass caught elsewhere in a traditional Georgian manner—his parents none the wiser. He fished his new charges hard. After a tough start, he began to improve his technique and eventually caught each fish several times a day. And then, as fish will do, they began to smarten up. At first they became a little tougher to catch, then impossible to catch—the slightest movement around the pool sending them to shiver in fear by the drain. Frank was finally reduced to blind casting to them from behind the fence which housed the pool pumps and filters.

Spring arrived, and Frank was preparing to unstock his pond thereby slipping another fast one past the parents, but his bass had done the natural thing—spawned. And one day his mother passed the pool to see, not a couple of bass, but hundreds hovering over the pool steps or, more accurately, spawning beds. For the first time (but as he is now a fishing guide, not the last time), Frank was made to suffer for his sport.

BY THE WAY, I'LL BE BRINGING MY DOG TODAY," IS A SENTENCE THAT ASSURES YOU AN ENEMY OR TWO ON A FISHING TRIP. AND WHILE IT IS TRUE THAT EVEN THE BEST-MANNERED POOCH WILL OCCASIONALLY SCREW UP A FISH, THE PLEASURE OF HIS COMPANY USUALLY OUTWEIGHS THE ODD LOST CHANCE—BRINGING TO MIND CHURCHILL'S PRONOUNCEMENT ON BRANDY, "IN THE END, I GOT MORE OUT OF IT THAN IT GOT OUT OF ME."

Silver Creek

Red Cliffs, Big Wood River

Silver Creek

TO THE FISHERMAN LIVING IN THE SUN VALLEY AREA OF IDAHO, THESE TWO STREAMS ARE HOME WATER. EVERY ANGLER LIKES THE IDEA THAT THERE IS A PIECE OF WATER NOT FAR FROM HIS HOME ON WHICH HE ENJOYS THE ADVANTAGE OF SUPERIOR KNOWLEDGE. HOME WATER MAY BE BAYOU LAFOUCHE, A FARM POND OR SILVER CREEK, BUT IT IS PROBABLY THE PLACE WHERE ONE FISHES MOST AND GENERALLY THE PLACE WHERE ONE FISHES BEST.

T HE NOVICE FLY
FISHERMAN OFTEN HAS
QUESTIONS CONCERNING THE
BEST TIME OF YEAR TO PLAN
HIS VENTURES AND ABOUT
THE EFFECT OF VARIOUS
WEATHER CONDITIONS ON
THE FISHING. AS HE
BECOMES MORE SEASONED,
HE OFTEN LEARNS TO
DISREGARD THE TECHNICAL
ANSWERS IN FAVOR OF THE
TIME-HONORED RULE THAT
THE BEST TIME TO GO
FISHING IS WHENEVER YOU
CAN.

Upper Yellowstone

TROUT THAT ONE MIGHT ENCOUNTER IN THE RIVERS OF THE WEST COME IN TWO DISTINCT VARIETIES, HATCHERY AND WILD—THE LATTER BEING IN ALL WAYS SUPERIOR TO THE FORMER. HATCHERY FISH ARE RAISED IN LONG CONCRETE TANKS BY THE THOUSANDS. WHEN RELEASED INTO OUR RIVERS, THEY COMPETE WITH THE WILD FISH. IT IS A BATTLE THE HATCHERY FISH INVARIABLY WIN. THE WILD TROUT NEEDS THE SENSE OF SPACE ABOUT HIM, THE SECURITY OF TERRITORY. THESE NEEDS ARE LOST IN THE CONCRETE CRIBS OF THE HATCHERY FISH, WHO GLADLY TRAVEL ABOUT IN PACKS BUMPING OUT WHATEVER GETS IN THEIR WAY. AS HATCHERY FISH ARE INHERENTLY POORLY PREPARED TO SURVIVE IN THE WILD OVER THE LONG HAUL, THEY DO LITTLE FOR A RIVER BUT DIMINISH THE STRENGTH OF THE GENE POOL. IT IS THE GROWING REALIZATION OF MOST TROUT ANGLERS THAT THE HEALTHY FUTURE OF THE SPORT LIES NOT IN PRODUCING MORE AND MORE HATCHERY FISH BUT RATHER IN PROVIDING SUITABLE HABITAT AND PROTECTION FOR WILD FISH.

Hatchery trout

Wild trout spawning

Brown drakes, Silver Creek

IT IS, OF COURSE, POSSIBLE TO FLY FISH FOR TROUT AND NEVER USE A FLY WHICH IMITATES AQUATIC INSECT LIFE. YOU CAN TOSS STREAMERS MEANT TO FOOL FISH INTO BELIEVING THEY ARE DINING ON THEIR BRETHREN. LARGER FISH, REQUIRING A GOOD PROTEIN POP PER EFFORT, ARE OFTEN GOOD STREAMER TARGETS. OTHER AQUATIC LIFE FORMS (SHRIMP, CRAYFISH) ALSO FIGURE INTO THE TROUT'S DIET. OR YOU MIGHT TRY TERRESTRIALS, THINGS THAT OUGHT NOT TO BE IN THE WATER BUT OFTEN ARE—GRASSHOPPERS, ANTS, CRICKETS. AND THEN WE HAVE ATTRACTORS, ROYAL WULFF BEING A RENOWNED EXAMPLE. THESE IMITATE NOTHING IN PARTICULAR BUT WORK VERY WELL AT TIMES, SORT OF THE OSSO BUCCO OF TROUT FOOD—WE'RE NOT SURE WHAT IT IS, BUT WE LIKE IT. BEYOND THIS WE ENTER THE TAWDRY WORLD OF THE SAN JUAN WORM, THE FLORESCENT EGG AND THE MOUSE PATTERN.

DESPITE THESE ALTERNATIVES, INSECTS IN ONE FORM OR ANOTHER REMAIN FAR AND AWAY THE TROUT'S NUMBER ONE FOOD SOURCE. TROUT INGEST INSECTS AS NYMPHS, LARVAE, PUPAE, EMERGERS, DUNS, SPINNERS. THERE ARE FLIES TIED TO IMITATE ALL OF THESE STAGES—THESE FLIES COMPRISE THE MOST FORMIDABLE AND ENJOYABLE METHOD OF TAKING TROUT ON A FLY ROD.

~

THE BROWN DRAKE HATCH OF SILVER CREEK IS A PHENOMENON NOT WELL SERVED BY THE THRASHING OF LANGUAGE. IT NEEDS TO BE SEEN. WERE THERE NOT A FISH IN THE CREEK, IT WOULD STILL MERIT A TRIP. ADD THE BIG BROWNS AND, WELL . . .

~

A MORE MASSIVE CADDIS HATCH THAN THAT OF THE SOUTH FORK OF THE BOISE MIGHT WELL BE FOUND BUT NOT WITHOUT A FAIR AMOUNT OF LOOKING.

Caddis hatch, South Fork of the Boise

South Fork of the Boise

I T IS RUMORED THAT A CERTAIN FISHERMAN ONCE BECAME SO DESPONDENT THAT HE ACTUALLY REMAINED UNHAPPY WITH A FISH ON. FOR SUCH A PERSON THERE IS SIMPLY NO HOPE.

SPRING CREEKS

Henry's Fork

Warm Springs Creek, Idaho

Parson's Creek

THESE ELEGANT SPRING CREEKS RISE IN THE LOST RIVER VALLEY OF IDAHO. THE LOST RIVER RANGE (INCLUDING BORAH, THE STATE'S HIGHEST PEAK) PROVIDES A DRAMATIC BACKDROP FOR THE ANGLER FORTUNATE ENOUGH TO FISH THIS WATER.

Warm Springs Creek

R IPARIAN AREAS ARE COMPLEX AND VITALLY IMPORTANT ECOSYSTEMS. TO THE ANGLER, THEY ARE THE LAND WHICH MUST BE CROSSED TO REACH THE WATER; TO THE ECOLOGIST, THE LAND WHICH LARGELY DETERMINES THE QUALITY OF THE WATER. FISHERMEN HAVE SUPPORTED SIGNIFICANT IMPROVEMENTS IN RIPARIAN CONSERVATION, INCLUDING RESTRICTION OF LOGGING AND GRAZING NEAR RIVERBANKS.

Tolstoï, grandson of the Russian novelist, lives in Paris where he once owned the famous tackle shop Au Coin du Pêche. President of the Big Game Fishing Club de France, he travels the world pursuing all variety of game fish. On this afternoon Tolstoï was fly fishing on Silver Creek downstream from the Nature Conservancy Preserve. He is a spring creek fisherman of grace and finesse—a fisherman who makes you lay down your rod and just watch awhile.

Sacha Tolstoï on Silver Creek

Silver Creek, Old Larkin Ranch with metal bridge for irrigation equipment

"PINK ALBERT spinner
FALL" IS IDEAL ARCANE
TROUT TALK. WHAT WOULD A NON-
ANGLER MAKE OF THIS? WHO KNOWS?
PINK ALBERT IS, IN FACT, A MAYFLY
WHICH, WHEN RETURNING (FALLING)
TO THE RIVER TO DEPOSIT ITS EGGS,
IS KNOWN AS A SPINNER.

THIS TROUT WAS CAUGHT
DURING A PINK ALBERT SPINNER
FALL ON PARSON'S CREEK.

Pink Albert spinner fall, Parson's Creek

PALE MORNING DUNS COAST DOWN THE CREEK, BUNCHING UP IN EDDIES AND BENDS WHERE RAINBOWS SIP THEM AT THEIR LEISURE. AS WELL AS HAVING THE MOST LYRICAL OF BUG NAMES, THE PALE MORNING DUN PUTS ON ONE OF THE LOVELIEST OF HATCHES. SMALL YELLOW-BODIED INSECTS WITH DEAD WHITE UPLIFTED WINGS, A HATCH OF PALE MORNING DUNS RESEMBLES NOTHING SO MUCH AS A FLOTILLA OF TINY LEMON RIND SAILBOATS.

THIS RAINBOW WAS TAKEN DURING A PMD HATCH ON WARM SPRINGS CREEK.

Warm Springs Creek, Idaho

Spring creek rainbow

Warm Springs Creek

Warm Springs Creek

Warm Springs Creek

Silver Creek

Silver Creek, the Nature Conservancy, October

AN ORANGE LINE ZIPPING BACK AND FORTH ABOVE A TRANQUIL SPRING CREEK CAN MAKE ONE QUEASY. IT JUST SEEMS LIKE A BAD COLOR FOR SUCH WORK. ON THE OTHER HAND, THE TROUT AT SILVER CREEK'S NATURE CONSERVANCY PRESERVE, WHO SEE SO MANY FLY LINES IN A SEASON THEY CAN IDENTIFY THE BRAND IN THE AIR, AREN'T MUCH BOTHERED BY FLY LINE OF ANY COLOR. TO THEM A FLY LINE IS JUST PART OF THE SCENERY, LIKE A RED-WINGED BLACKBIRD. BUT TRY FLOATING ANY FUNKY-TIED, POORLY PRESENTED TRICO THROUGH ON 5X. THEY'LL SUCK DOWN THE TWENTY SPINNERS SURROUNDING YOUR OFFERING AND PASS YOURS BY WITH BARELY A GLANCE.

Brown drake hatch, Silver Creek, Old Larkin Ranch

T HE BROWN DRAKE HATCH STARTS AROUND DUSK AND CONTINUES WELL INTO THE NIGHT. THIS TROUT WAS HOOKED RELATIVELY EARLY IN THE GOING, AND ALTHOUGH THE DRAKES ARE NUMEROUS ON THE WATER HERE, THEY BECAME MUCH THICKER.

~

AS THE NIGHT PROGRESSES, THE FISHERMAN MUST SWITCH FROM VISUAL TO SONAR. HE CASTS NOT TO A SIGHTED RISE BUT RATHER TO THE SOUND OR HINT OF A RISE—OR EVEN THE INTUITION OF ONE.

TWO OF THE
INTERESTING
CHALLENGES OF NIGHT
FLY FISHING ARE HOW
TO SEE TO TIE ON A FLY
OR A NEW TIPPET AND
WHEN TO STRIKE A FISH
INVISIBLE IN THE
DARKNESS. THE FIRST
CHALLENGE IS MET
WITH A SMALL
FLASHLIGHT HELD IN
YOUR MOUTH OR
ATTACHED TO YOUR
VEST. THE SECOND MAY
BE HANDLED WITH
GOOD LUCK, PLENTY OF
PRACTICE, OR A TERM
OF STUDY IN TIBET.

FREESTONES

&TAILWATERS

Brook trout

THE UPPER BIG SANDY IS LOADED WITH BROOK TROUT. IT IS DIFFICULT TO IMAGINE A MORE IDEAL BEGINNERS' STREAM. THE RIVER AND SURROUNDING LANDSCAPE ARE BEAUTIFUL, AND YOU *WILL* CATCH FISH. FOR THE SEASONED FISHERMAN, IT'S A GREAT PLACE TO BREAK OUT THE ONE WEIGHT. FARTHER DOWN, THE RIVER SUPPORTS A GOOD POPULATION OF BROWN TROUT, SOME OF WHICH FIND THEIR WAY UPRIVER TO LIVE WITH THE BROOKIES.

THE BEAVER POND IS FLYWATER IN ITS MOST PEACEFUL FORM AS WELL AS A PRINCIPAL RESIDENCE OF THE EVER-HUNGRY BROOK TROUT—A COMBINATION OFFERING THE FLY FISHERMAN PLEASANT STRETCHES OF EXTREME TRANQUILITY MIXED WITH OCCASIONAL PAN-FISH VIOLENCE.

Big Sandy River, Wyoming

Big Sandy, Wyoming

This beautiful, inaptly named lake is part of the Big Sandy River system.

Mud Lake, Wyoming

F R E E S T O N E S

ENTERING A RIVER FOR THE FIRST TIME—ALL ANTICIPATION AND
MYSTERY AND POSSIBILITY.

Pit River, California

Madison River

F R E E S T O N E S

FORMED BY THE GIBBON AND THE FIREHOLE, THE MADISON RIVER RUNS OUT OF YELLOWSTONE PARK AND TRAVELS ACROSS A STRETCH OF MONTANA BEFORE CONTRIBUTING ITS WATERS TO THE MISSOURI RIVER. THE MADISON IS SOMETHING OF A MONUMENT IN THE TROUT WORLD. FOR DECADES, EVEN ANGLERS FROM THE TROUTLESS MIDWEST AND SOUTH WERE REARED ON MADISON RIVER TALES WHICH TRICKLED DOWN TO THEM THROUGH THE PAGES OF *SPORTS AFIELD* AND *FIELD & STREAM.* ALTHOUGH INCREASED FISHING PRESSURE HAS SIGNIFICANTLY ALTERED THE EXPERIENCE OVER THE YEARS, IN THE HEARTS AND MINDS OF MANY AN ANGLER, FLYWATER IS STILL DEFINED BY AND MEASURED AGAINST THE MADISON RIVER.

Upper Yellowstone River

ASK A FLYFISHERMAN WHAT ATTRACTS HIM TO THE SPORT, AND YOU ARE LIKELY TO HEAR HIM SAY "THE GREAT PLACES IT TAKES YOU." ONE OF THOSE PLACES IS THE UPPER YELLOWSTONE RIVER. FISHING THE YELLOWSTONE, ABOVE THE LAKE, FOR A FULL WEEK WITHOUT SEEING ANOTHER SOUL PUTS IN PERSPECTIVE THE NATIONAL TREASURE THAT IS YELLOWSTONE PARK.

~

THIS SPOT ON THE UPPER YELLOWSTONE RIVER CAN BE REACHED BY COMBINING A LONG BOAT RIDE ACROSS YELLOWSTONE LAKE WITH A 10-MILE HIKE.

Upper Yellowstone River

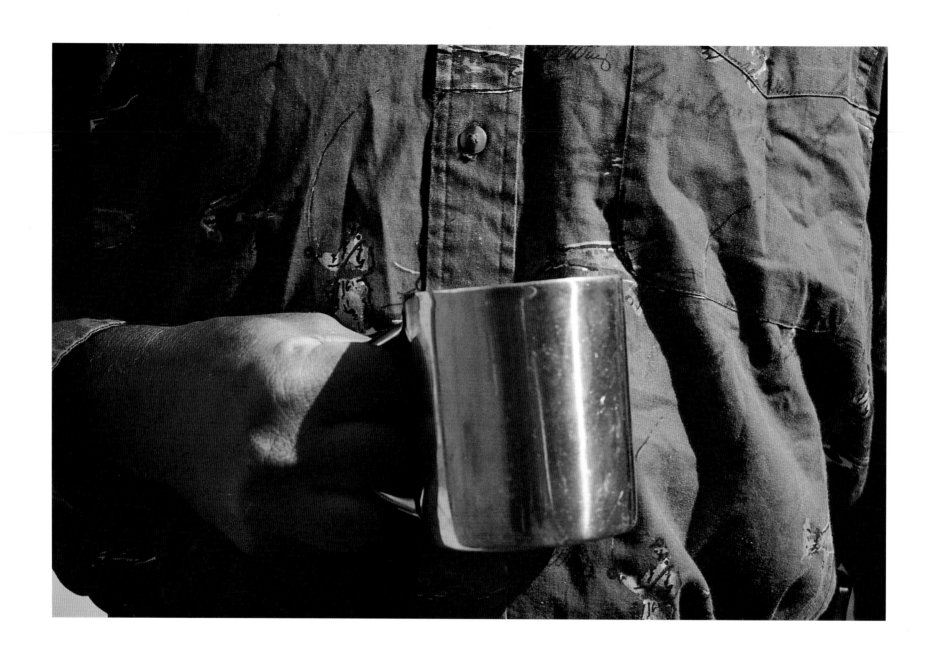

Yellowstone cutthroat

ABUSE AND DERISION APLENTY HAS BEEN HEAPED UPON THE YELLOWSTONE CUTTHROAT. AND THERE IS NO DENYING THAT IN TERMS OF FIGHT AND INTELLIGENCE, THE YELLOWSTONE LAGS BEHIND HIS RAINBOW AND BROWN BROTHERS. THE FIGHT OF THE YELLOWSTONE MOST RESEMBLES THE THROES OF AN INSOMNIAC IN A TWIN BED. HE COMES TO THE SURFACE, STAYS IN ONE PLACE AND FLOPS AROUND AS YOU REEL HIM HOME. AND AS TO INTELLIGENCE, IT IS POSSIBLE TO STICK AND MISS A FISH TWICE ONLY TO HAVE HIM RISE DETERMINEDLY A THIRD TIME. SELECTIVE THEY ARE NOT. ASK A KNOWLEDGEABLE ANGLER WHAT PATTERN TO TRY ON A YELLOWSTONE AND HE'S LIKELY TO REPLY, "SOMETHING YOU CAN SEE."

ON THE OTHER HAND, WHAT'S SO AWFUL ABOUT A FISH THAT COMES WILLINGLY TO A DRY FLY?

AND THIS DRAMATICALLY BEAUTIFUL AMERICAN NATIVE IS CAUGHT IN MAJESTIC, UNDAMMED AMERICAN WATERS. PLUS THESE FISH HAVE A BIT OF SIZE. YOU CAN FISH FOR A WEEK ON THE UPPER YELLOWSTONE AND CATCH NOTHING SMALLER THAN 15 INCHES AND LITERALLY HUNDREDS OVER THAT LENGTH. IN THE END, THE SIN OF BEING SOMEWHAT LESS SPORTY THAN THE RAINBOW OR BROWN IS MORE THAN ATONED FOR BY THEIR WILLINGNESS, THEIR BEAUTY, AND THE ESSENTIAL RIGHTNESS OF THEIR PRESENCE IN THE RIVER.

S IGNIFICANT REWARDS ACCRUE TO THE FISHERMAN
WHO RISES BEFORE DAWN, GULPS HIS COFFEE, AND
BECOMES FULLY AWAKE ONLY AS HE WADES INTO THE COLD WATER.

BENEFITS CAN INCLUDE A MORNING HATCH, SOLITUDE, AND
WITNESSING THE DAWN OF THE DAY.

THE TAILWATER STRETCH OF THE MISSOURI IS SOMETIMES
CALLED MONTANA'S BIGGEST "SPRING CREEK." THE EXCELLENT
FISHING HERE IS NO LONGER A WELL-KEPT SECRET, BUT THERE IS
STILL AMPLE ROOM FOR DRY FLY FISHING TO PODS OF REMARKABLY
STRONG RAINBOWS.

THE BLACK CANYON OF THE GUNNISON OFFERS GRANDEUR,
BEAUTIFUL RAINBOW TROUT, AND A FAIR SHOT AT CARDIAC
ARREST ON THE CLIMB OUT.

Rainbow, Gunnison River

Gunnison River, Colorado

FREESTONES

Brook trout

THE LITTLE WOOD MOVES THROUGH THE DESERT IN LONG RIFFLE SECTIONS THAT LEAD TO DEEP POOLS BRACKETED BY ROCK OUTCROPS. THESE POOLS DROP INTO SMOOTH RUNS WHICH EVENTUALLY FORM RIFFLES COMPLETING THE CYCLE. THE LAVA ROCK BOTTOM MAKES THE RIVER WADABLE IN FLORSHEIMS.

Little Wood River, Idaho

CERTAIN RIVERS SEEM TO DELIVER US AT ONCE BACK TO CHILDHOOD—TO SIMPLICITY AND WONDER, TO THE SURE SENSE THAT THIS WORLD IS THE RIGHT PLACE FOR A FISHERMAN.

Little Wood

Little Wood

Quake Lake

QUAKE LAKE IS A GREAT BULGE IN THE MADISON CREATED BY THE EARTHQUAKE OF 1959. A SHALLOW SAND SPIT RUNS A COUPLE OF HUNDRED YARDS DOWN THE MIDDLE OF THE LAKE. WADE DOWN THIS SPIT AND YOU CAN CAST EITHER BACK TOWARD THE SHORE OR OUT INTO THE LAKE. AN AMPLE BAETIS HATCH COMES OFF HERE—ESPECIALLY ON CLOUDY DAYS.

THE BRAIDED WATER BELOW QUAKE LAKE HOLDS SOME VERY LARGE AND LIVELY TROUT.

T HIS PICTURESQUE FREESTONE RUNS DOWN FROM THE BITTERROOT MOUNTAINS INTO IDAHO. THE KELLY IS A SUPERB WESTSLOPE CUTTHROAT FISHERY BUT THE SEASON IS SHORT—LATE SUMMER AND, IN SOME YEARS, EARLY FALL.

Kelly Creek

THE SMITH RIVER FLOWS FROM SOUTH TO NORTH BETWEEN THE BIG BELT AND LITTLE BELT MOUNTAINS OF IVAN DOIG'S "HOUSE OF SKY" COUNTRY. FISHING IT REQUIRES A FOUR- OR FIVE-DAY FLOAT OF ALMOST 60 MILES. THE RIVER SNAKES ALONG HYPNOTICALLY IN A SEEMINGLY ENDLESS NUMBER OF BENDS AGAINST HIGH CANYON WALLS.

Smith River, Montana

Smith River

IN THE BEGINNING, THE GEAR MEANT JUST ABOUT EVERYTHING—PROBABLY BECAUSE IT WAS THE FIRST ASPECT OF FLY FISHING WE COULD UNDERSTAND AND CONTROL. OUR VISION OF THE AUTHENTIC FLY FISHERMAN INCLUDED THE FULLY-STOCKED FISHING VEST AND, OF COURSE, NEOPRENE WADERS (WALKING IN WATER WITHOUT GETTING WET WAS LIKE BREATHING ON THE MOON). BUT SOME FISHERMEN FIND THERE IS NOTHING ESSENTIAL IN THE VEST THAT WON'T FIT IN A SHIRT POCKET, AND THAT, GIVEN A WATER TEMPERATURE IN THE MID-50S OR MORE, "WET" WADING IS PREFERABLE.

A POD OF FISH ON THE FAR SIDE OF THE RIVER UNDER A ROCK WALL ROSE TO THE CADDIS HATCH. THE FISHERMEN WERE SEPARATED FROM THEIR QUARRY BY A DAUNTING WIDTH OF UNWADABLE WATER DEMANDING A STEELHEAD-LENGTH CAST AND A BEHEMOTH MEND— ALL THIS, IF PROPERLY EXECUTED, WOULD RESULT IN A DECENT DRIFT OF THREE OR FOUR FEET. IN OTHER WORDS, ABOUT AS MUCH FUN AS YOU CAN HAVE WITH A FLY ROD. THE FOUR FISHERMEN ROTATED THROUGH—GUIDES AND SPORTS ALIKE TAKING THEIR SHOTS ONE AT A TIME.

South Fork of the Boise

San Miguel, March

THE SAN MIGUEL RIVER, ONE OF ONLY TWO UNDAMMED COLORADO FREESTONES, HAS 40 MILES OF FLYWATER HOLDING BROOK TROUT, RAINBOWS, BROWNS AND CUTTHROAT.

San Juan River

THIS EVENING SCENE WITH ITS LONE FISHERMAN MAY NOT LOOK FAMILIAR TO THOSE WHO HAVE FISHED THE SECTION OF THE SAN JUAN RIVER IMMEDIATELY BELOW THE NAVAJO RESERVOIR. THE "QUALITY WATER," AS IT IS CALLED, HAS BECOME ONE OF THE MOST CROWDED PIECES OF TROUT RIVER IN THE WEST. BUT EVEN FISHERMEN WHO ABHOR COMPETING FOR SPACE ARE DRAWN TO THIS RIVER FROM TIME TO TIME BY THE IMPRESSIVE NUMBERS OF BIG RAINBOWS. AS YOGI BERRA SAID, "NO ONE GOES THERE ANY MORE—IT'S TOO CROWDED."

Green River, Utah

A VERY BEAUTIFUL CANYON RIVER WITH LOTS OF FISH, THE GREEN RIVER, LIKE THE SAN JUAN, IS OFTEN JUST TOO CROWDED IN THE UPPER STRETCHES.

MAGIC RESERVOIR SUPPORTS A HEALTHY POPULATION OF HATCHERY TROUT WITH IMPECCABLE CREDENTIALS AT THE TABLE. LEAVING HIS DOG PARTRIDGE ON THE SHORE, JACK HEMINGWAY WADED OUT TO HARVEST A FEW.

Magic Reservoir, Idaho

H AT CREEK
THROWS A
SALMON FLY HATCH
THAT COULD MAKE
EVEN A MONTANA
GUIDE CONSIDER
VISITING CALIFORNIA.

Salmon fly

Hat Creek, California

Drift boat fishing, rainy day

I T IS, OF COURSE, A GOOD IDEA TO FISH IN THE RAIN AS WELL AS IN THE SUN. IT IS
ALSO A GOOD IDEA TO PUT YOUR PERMITS IN A WATERPROOF BAG.

F R E E S T O N E S

BROWN TROUT WERE FIRST STOCKED IN THE FIREHOLE IN 1890—
A HUNDRED GENERATIONS' WORTH OF ADAPTATION. THESE
TROUT NOT ONLY SURVIVE BUT ACTUALLY PREFER THE INORDINATELY WARM
WATER OF THE FIREHOLE (MID 70S IN SUMMER).

Firehole River

Dolores River

COLORADO'S DOLORES RIVER, BELOW McPHEE RESERVOIR, IS A SMALL TAILWATER WITH 12 MILES OF CATCH-AND-RELEASE WATER HOLDING LARGE BUT SELECTIVE RAINBOWS, BROWNS, AND CUTTHROATS THAT CAN TEST THE ANGLER'S PATIENCE. DURING THE WINTER MONTHS, THE UPPER SIX MILES ARE BEST REACHED BY MOUNTAIN BIKE.

WILDLIFE IN YELLOWSTONE PARK OFTEN SEEMS ALMOST TAME—A MISCONCEPTION WHICH LEADS TO A NUMBER OF INJURED TOURISTS EACH YEAR.

Little Firehole

A FISHERMAN ON THE ROAD MIGHT PASS THE NIGHT IN ANYTHING FROM A SLEEPING BAG TO A COZY LODGE SPORTING AN EXCELLENT WINE CELLAR. BETWEEN THESE POLES LIES A VAST SEA OF MOTELS, HOTELS, AND CABINS-FOR-RENT. THESE RANGE FROM SHELTERS WHICH WILL BARELY SUSTAIN LIFE ON A COLD NIGHT TO ROOMS OF GREAT COMFORT AND CHARM—THE WAGON WHEEL MOTEL IN MacKAY IS AMONG THE LATTER.

Wagon Wheel Motel, MacKay, Idaho

S T E E L H E A D

Salmon River, October

FLY FISHING THE STEELHEAD RUNS OF
NORTH AMERICAN RIVERS REQUIRES A
PATIENCE BORDERING ON MENTAL INSTABILITY. CAST
AFTER CAST AFTER CAST, DAYS CAN, AND OFTEN DO,
PASS WITHOUT SO MUCH AS A TUG. THEN COMES THE
SUDDEN STRIKE OF A STEELHEAD—AND ALL THOSE
DAYS OF WAITING MELT INTO A SINGLE MOMENT.

Salmon River

Fog over the Salmon River

THE SALMON IS THE LONGEST RIVER CONTAINED ENTIRELY WITHIN ONE STATE (IDAHO) AND ALSO THE LONGEST UNDAMMED RIVER IN AMERICA.

Two-handed caster

TWO-HANDED RODS ARE BECOMING INCREASINGLY POPULAR FOR STEELHEADING. THE ADVANTAGES ARE SEVERAL: GREATER DISTANCE, LESS FALSE CASTING (MORE TIME WITH THE FLY IN THE WATER), A LONGER WEAPON FOR PLAYING THE FISH AROUND OBSTACLES, AND, IN COLD WEATHER, THE ABILITY TO FISH IN GLOVES OR EVEN MITTENS. FOR THE FISHERMAN BOTHERED BY TENNIS ELBOW, THE TWO-HANDED ROD CAN BE AN ESPECIALLY WELCOME RELIEF.

Fly fisherman, Salmon River

THERE IS A METHOD OF SPIN FISHING FOR STEELHEAD KNOWN AS SIDE PLANING— A TECHNIQUE WHICH FLY FISHERMEN FIND GENERALLY ODIOUS. SIDE PLANERS, ON THE OTHER HAND, TAKE A SORT OF BEMUSED ATTITUDE TOWARD FLY FISHERMEN. WHY GET IN THE RIVER AND EXPEND ALL THAT ENERGY? THE SIDE PLANER SIMPLY TOSSES HIS CONSIDERABLE RIG OUT WHERE THE FISH LIE, SETS UP AN ALUMINUM CHAIR AND WAITS IN COMFORT.

THE FLY FISHERMAN AND THE SIDE PLANER SHARE AN ULTIMATE OBJECTIVE —TO CATCH FISH. BUT FOR THE FLY FISHERMAN, THE STYLE IN WHICH THAT OBJECTIVE IS REACHED IS ITSELF A CERTAIN PLEASURE.

Steelhead

118   S T E E L H E A D

Cornfield by the Salmon River

Snake River

THE SNAKE IS BIG WATER, RATHER INTIMIDATING ON FIRST VIEWING. THE SHORT STRETCH BETWEEN ASOTIN, WASHINGTON, AND THE GRANDE RONDE OFFERS MORE LIKELY STEELHEAD LIES THAN ONE COULD COVER IN A WEEK.

Casting for steelhead, Snake River

Horses, Thompson River

Hemingway, Grande Ronde

Grande Ronde steelhead

JACK HEMINGWAY TOOK THIS HEN ON THE RONDE WITH A FLY OF
HIS DESIGN, THE CAPTAIN JACK.

Grande Ronde, Schumaker

THE GRANDE RONDE IS A STEELHEAD RIVER BUILT ON THE MODEL OF A TROUT STREAM —A COMFORTABLE RIVER MORE INTIMATE THAN MOST STEELHEAD VENUES. IN A NORMAL YEAR, YOU CAN WADE ACROSS THE RONDE HERE AND THERE WITHOUT TOO MUCH DISTRESS. THE RONDE RUNS OUT OF NORTHEAST OREGON INTO WASHINGTON AND DOWN A DRAMATIC CANYON TO EMPTY INTO THE SNAKE RIVER.

A CONGA LINE OF FISHERMEN PROCEED AT A CAST-AND-STEP PACE DOWN GRAVEYARD HOLE. THE FIRST FELLOW IS INTO A GOOD STEELHEAD, ONE WHICH WILL SHORTLY STRAIGHTEN HIS HOOK AND SWIM OFF WITH THE CASUAL DISDAIN THAT THOMPSON RIVER STEELHEAD SHOW FOR INADEQUATE TACKLE.

Graveyard Hole

Graveyard Hole, Thompson River, British Columbia

NAMED FOR THE HOTEL OPPOSITE, THE STEELHEAD INN, THIS RUN IS TYPICAL OF THE THOMPSON. IT IS A LONG, PRODUCTIVE STRETCH OF FLYWATER THAT CAN TAKE HALF A DAY TO FISH.

Hotel Run

TRAINS ARE AS COMMON AS MERGANSERS ON THE THOMPSON. THE CANADIAN PACIFIC RUNS DOWN ONE SIDE OF THE RIVER AND THE CANADIAN NATIONAL DOWN THE OTHER. TRAINS PASS THE TOWN OF SPENCES BRIDGE THROUGHOUT THE NIGHT, GIVING THE BEDS OF THE STEELHEAD INN A GENTLE SHAKE.

Grease Hole

THE "GREASE" IN GREASE HOLE MOST LIKELY REFERS TO THE CONDITION OF THE BOTTOM IN THIS STEELHEAD RUN. HOWEVER, THOUGH NOT AN EASY WADE, IT IS ONE OF THE LESS TREACHEROUS ON THE THOMPSON—A RIVER WHOSE BOTTOM TRULY MERITS THE "GREASED BOWLING BALLS" CLICHÉ. IF YOU HAVE EVER WONDERED WHY YOU BOUGHT THOSE STREAM CLEATS AND THAT WADING STAFF, COME TO THE THOMPSON FOR ENLIGHTENMENT.

FLYWATER FOR THE FUTURE

MIKE CROCKETT

As a fly fishing neophyte I was obsessed, spending every possible minute casting the fly, marching upstream, and carefully counting the fish I hooked. I fished until I was totally exhausted, until Andy begged, then demanded, to go home, or until complete darkness fell—usually whichever came last. Over the years, I have evolved a more mellow approach. Now I can pick my spots, watch the stream before wading in, sacrifice the pleasure of the eight-inch trout to improve the chances for the bigger one at the head of the pool, and, sometimes, even finish my lunch before charging back into the river.

Those who have experienced a similar angling maturation understand that simply putting in the hours and flailing the water with the maximum number of casts does not necessarily guarantee results. It helps to be fishing where there are fish and with a fly they'll eat. On one of those early fishing days, I ran into a young man who had just fished the same river I had. He was wearing a smile and a sunburn, and had a few dry flies stuck in his baseball cap. When he noticed I had been fishing, he shared a gratuitous report of his fabulous day on the river. Before this encounter I would have described my own day as a pleasant one, even though I had fished hard with unspectacular results. Now, I am not in this sport to compete with anyone but myself, but his story must have made me take a fresh look at how I had done on that particular day. Mentally wrestling with this for a few moments while our conversation turned to small talk, I finally couldn't keep from asking about his choice of flies and

about which stretch of the river he had fished. I cannot remember his exact response, but in essence it was: "Can't tell you."

The sport is notorious for lies and for secrets of all flavors. It is a dear friend indeed who honestly shares the exact location of a good fish, a good pool, or a productive fly, and even when he does, he will most certainly ask that you not repeat it to anyone else. There is a simple reason for all this selfish secrecy: an explosion of new anglers in pursuit of a shrinking resource. In just the eight years I have been fly fishing, the number of fly fishermen has, by some estimates, more than tripled. In one sense, this growth is a very positive development; after all, ours is a society bound increasingly to desks, computer terminals, television screens, and sofas. The average American spends just two percent of the day outdoors. And for those who make their living guiding, supplying, and otherwise accommodating fly fishermen, it is a rewarding time to be in business. But for the individual angler, whose goals may include solitude and relaxation, a noticeable increase in fishermen working his home water is cause for anxiety. It is with similar mixed emotions that we have published this book. On the one hand, as with most of you, we feel such enthusiasm for this wonderful activity we cannot help telling our friends and taking them with us. On the other, picturing our favorite pools (can't tell you) overcrowded with anglers and underpopulated by trout is most disheartening.

Our hope is that some may ask what can be done to protect this great resource of flywater for use by future generations. One of the ironies of this ambivalence many of us feel about promoting our sport is that each new competitor for our fishing space will probably be a new convert to the cause of protecting our rivers. Fly fishing is a springboard to new awareness of the workings of river systems, weather, geography, and wildlife and nature in general. And, though all but the most myopic fishheads would concede that fly fishing in itself is no more important to the human condition than beach volleyball, stock car racing, or any other recreational pursuit, the unique aspect of fly fishing is that the condition of the fisherman's playing field is such a reliable indicator of the health of the planet.

As Jack Hemingway can tell us, there have been tremendous changes, many of them adverse, in the quality of the fly fishing experience since he was introduced to the sport. However, we must start from where we are: the trout, the streams, and the beauty are still there. The photographs in this book make an adequate case that the magic of the flywater resource still exists, and that it is worthy of preservation.

What are the threats to flywater? First, and most obvious, there are great increases in fishing pressure as a result of the rapidly increasing popularity of the sport and, in the longer term, because of rising world population, now projected to double every forty years. For many of us the only sensible method of dealing with the increasing fishing pressure in the short term is simply to resolve any doubts about when to go fishing in favor of going today, but we also have to promote, as short-term solutions, such strategies as better streamside etiquette, better treatment of fish when they are being released, and reducing our wading through spawning areas.

But what about the long term? Is our favorite recreation doomed? Will the home stream run bone-dry before the grandchildren have a chance to fish it? Will there be a decent opportunity to catch a trout only in the elbow-to-elbow company of other fishermen (a scene already played out on a number of western rivers)? Will only those wealthy enough to own their own spring creeks enjoy fly fishing as we know it today? If the answers to these questions, based on current trends, are Yes, then what should we, as concerned fishheads, do to change those trends?

Certainly, we should continue to send our dues and give our time to Trout Unlimited and other conservation groups, and to fight the familiar problems of overgrazing, poor logging practices, water pollution, overdevelopment, overfishing in the oceans, dam building and other water management practices biased in favor of economic development at the expense of the natural environment. We should devote time and money to habitat restoration. We can support the catch-and-release ethic.

But while we attack these symptoms, it is important to recognize that there is a root cause of most of the threats to flywater and, for that matter, of many larger social and environmental problems: unchecked growth in the population of the planet.

Everything we do to promote the conservation of natural resources can be more than offset by population growth. Conversely, slowing the growth in the number of users of the planet contributes to many goals at once. Preserving flywater and saving the habitat of our favorite creatures may be far down the list of those goals in a universal sense, but it is on the list. Surely it would help to stop pretending we can isolate the trout stream from the effects of macroeconomic growth by putting a wall around the river and pulling up the ladder. Focusing on population growth as a strategy for protecting flywater may seem a very long-term and remote solution—because it is. But in the long term it is the only solution. Breaching the carrying capacity of the planet will affect flywater and every other resource.

Of course, discouraging parenthood and its joys would be as perverse as discouraging fly fishing. The solution instead is a much greater allocation of funding for education in family planning at all levels. Even as one who has had a delightful experience with parenthood, I am convinced that the obligations of bringing a new person into the world are rarely, if ever, fully understood. And on an entirely different level of educational focus, we have children bearing children without even knowing how that happens. We can no longer allow religious and moral concerns about sexuality and abortion to interfere with a greater effort toward the goal of making every child born on the planet one who is wanted and loved by parents—parents who made the most fully-informed decision possible. Achieving this goal would finish a good many troubles before they start.

One of the marvelous aspects of fly fishing is its ability to transport the practitioner from what may otherwise be a relatively serious kind of existence, full of concerns about the future and regrets for the past, into the present. Concerns about overcrowding aside, we should take all 5 billion folks fly fishing; by making them all fishing buddies, we would defuse most of the world's distress. It is simply not possible to stand in a river with fly rod in hand and look much beyond a rising trout. And of course, the best news is that, today, this beautiful resource we call flywater is still with us; if there is concern for its future, all the better. It's not likely to interfere with today's fishing. We hope you've enjoyed the book. See you on the stream.

ACKNOWLEDGMENTS

GRATEFUL APPRECIATION TO ALL THOSE WHO HELPED US IN THE PRODUCTION OF THIS BOOK: STEVE BRYANT, J. D. LOVE, SACHA TOLSTOÏ, RICK WELLE, DAN HULL, BLAKE QUINN, JO ANN & JULIAN GANZ, BUTCH HARPER, LEITA & BILL HAMILL, MIKE BAY, PAT ELAM, BARRY HOOD, DENA & BOB HUDSON, JOHN VICKERS, MIKE GEARY, JASON JONAS, KIRK VANVALKENBURGH, CAROL HARALSON, ROSS LIVINGSTON, PAULETTE MILLICHAP, COUNCIL OAK BOOKS, SCOTT SCHNEBLY, FRANK SMETHURST, CLARK SHAFER, BART QUESNELL, RICH SPALDING, BILL WHITE, TERRY RING, ROB FOLGER, GEORGE SINGER, JODY PARKER, ROGER WHEELER, ANGELA & JACK HEMINGWAY, ANDREA KNORR, PAULA McCLINTOCK, H. A. MOORE, HERB BEATTIE, DAVID RIGGS, GARY NEAL, JERRY PARKHURST, TERRY TURNER, SCOTT FLYROD COMPANY, NICK LYONS, DAVID BISHOP, KAREN DAVIDSON, KEITH WRIGHT.

142